Those Who Favor Fire,

Those Who Pray To Fire

other books by EMP

More Poems About Purple Wizards and Neon-Bright Exceptionalisms
by Jason Preu

A Banner Year
by Iris Appelquist

What We Face Walking Out The Front Door
by Zophia McDougal

The Former Lives of Saints
by Ezhno Martin & Damian Rucci

Don't Lose Your Head
by Jeanette Powers

TEN-FOOT-TALL AND BULLET-PROOF
by Jason Ryberg

Beautiful Earthworms & Abominable Stars
by Ezhno Martin & Jeanette Powers

As I Watch You Fade
by James Benger

Those Who Favor Fire, Those Who Pray To Fire

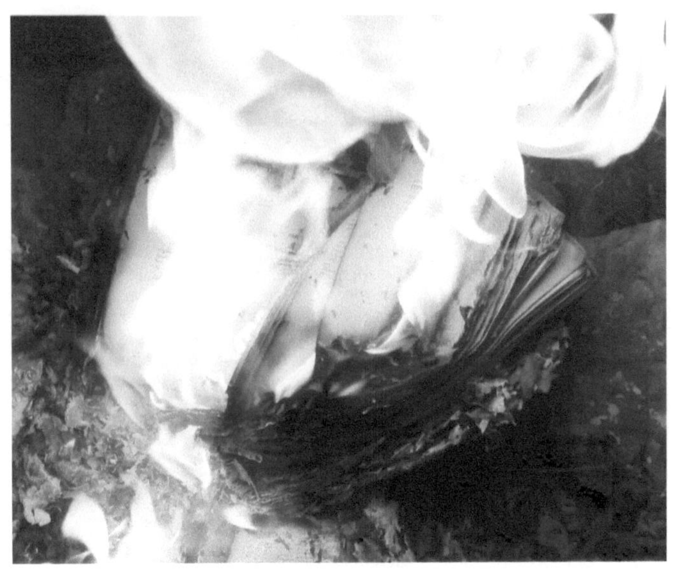

poems by

Ben Brindise &
Justin Karcher

EMP

Kansas City, MO

http://www.empbooks.com

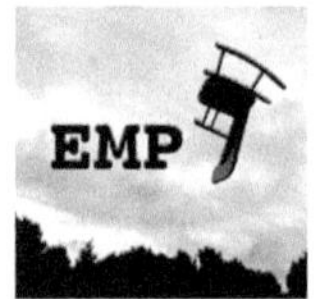

First Edition

ISBN: 978-0-9985077-9-8

LOC: 2017963820

10 19 33 34 6 11 1973

Design and Layout: Ezhno Martín

Cover Photo: Acatana (if you've been playing the home game, you realize we've really been liking Germans with one name)

Edits: Ezhno Martín, Ben Brindise, Justin Karcher and Jeanette Powers

Those Who Favor Fire

Ben Brindise

Those Who Pray to Fire

Justin Karcher

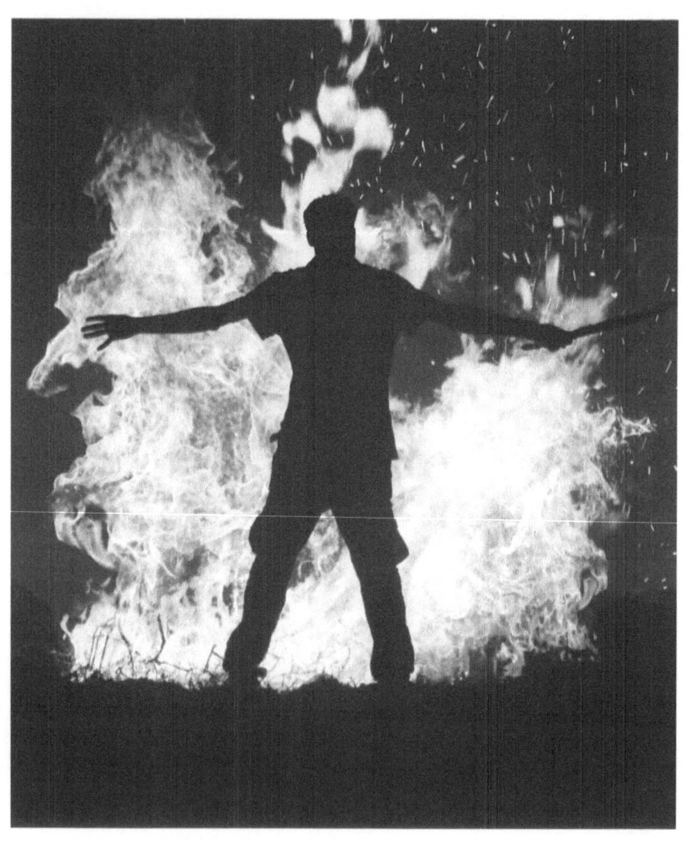

Those Who Favor Fire

these aren't mine

I woke up with a swollen throat
as if it wished to remind me
that a voice rattled inside

there's a suggestion box at work
covered in wrapping paper
and ribbon
that I think wants
to catch flames

I've gotten so lazy
I take other poets' imagery
and I want to stitch it into a wardrobe
to wear as a costume

I don't know where my hands went
these aren't mine

it all feels like work
the kind you do to get through to that something
you've fallen in love with
the idea of falling in love with
in a world where they never invented
the things you love

which is to say
these bandages have been growing
and placed the right way
make me a mummy

the kind that don't scratch
last rites inside sarcophagi

which is to say
there are days when words
feel as useful as kindling
stuffed inside a suggestion box
that no one looked at
until it was on fire

which is to say
when my throat swells
sometimes I think it's to remind me
that all faucets
eventually run dry

a room full of mannequins

a circle of blank faces
soft eyes, block hands
stances that never change
even when the water comes

sometimes it feels like Hertel Avenue
that one time it flooded
right up to everyone's porches

when anything kept in boxes
basements, under stairs, put away
was brought to the curb

had to be thrown out
had become a health hazard

they stare unaffected
from stitched together sockets
no matter how loud
they don't remove the pins
from their eyes

sitting on those wood slat piers
that splinter in your shoes
it's all right—
the wind coming off the water
keeps flies from landing on your cheeks
the rush of air fills your ears
blocks out screams from the kid
who dropped their ice cream overboard

you accept this as the best it'll ever be

sometimes speaking
is like shooting a fridge full of thermite
the last moment of pressure
pulled tight on the trigger
the instant explosion
that you can't get back

this lack of body language
has me feeling like a unicycle
playing the floor game
where the floor is my life's greatest ambition
and I'm in stasis above it in full spin
never finding traction

sometimes I sit in rooms
full of mannequins
and make sounds with my mouth
dictated by scratch marks
on the paper in front of me
I look up and project
the absolute nothingness that's inside me
onto their stocking faces
and nothing changes
the pins in their eyes push deeper

sometimes I sit in rooms full of mannequins
make sounds with my mouth
and wonder what the fuck
I'm doing

to burn a tree from the roots up

sometimes I take walks
I don't post about on Facebook
or write into poems
around a city I should know more about
but don't
I think about kicking the corner stone
of F. Scott Fitzgerald's childhood home
see how loose it is, see if I can really
leave a scar on this city

on these nights when it's past 2 a.m.
the only living breath comes
from the guy across the street
collecting cans from a blue bin
trying not to die
when I am my ugliest, truest self
with a gas-station cup full of kerosene
thirsty to burn down every treasure
you've ever had or chased

on these nights, when I'm wondering
how much kindling it would take
to burn a tree from the roots up
Bradbury whispers into my ear—
his voice crackles like splitting wood
hisses visages of helmeted heads
rank and file formations, smoke—

They'll come for the writers first

I shoo him away like an over protective mother
paw more crab grass and clover into clumps
mash them into the bark of a tree on Ashland
try to set them off with laser vision
but my eyes haven't been on fire in so long—
maybe they never were

maybe my community is just a collection
of pathological liars
committed to group therapy sessions
where we convince ourselves we're X-Men
with powers and nothing to do with them
when really we're all just mutants
who never pushed ourselves far enough
for our X-genes to trigger
just a bunch of half-cocked narcissists
who would welcome the fire like a spotlight
because the only thing more self-assuring
than pretending to be the hero
is playing the victim

my toe breaks on the hard surface
of the house's foundation
I feel it all the way
because I'm not drunk,
never really am, or need to be,
because the air in Buffalo
will fuck you up enough on its own

laced with pretend possibilities
and faux nostalgia
the only thing it's good for
is filling balloon animals

and the roots don't catch,
but it smokes a little
enough to let me know
that I really left the house
that I let night envelope me
like a poorly written cover letter
detailing a much better poem

The night feels younger than I have ever been
I drag the wreck of my foot along
the insides of the Clarks my mother bought me
filling up with blood,
it leaks out the shoe string holes
leaving a piece of myself on the sidewalks
as I make my way home

you become a flower in the least poetic way

my front porch is unbecoming
but I sit on its peeling stairs
and smoke cigarettes in gym shorts
with the waist string untied

they billow on my thighs like sagging skin,
but it suits the way I am on mornings after
the night before crawling up the garbage disposal
wants to die out in the open,
where everyone can see

a dream happened on this porch once
you were waiting on its steps for me
as I got home from work
you told me you were wrong,
that you were sorry
until I couldn't stop throwing up Kool-Aid

red syrup trapped between our sticking skin
little powder dots that didn't saturate in our hair
you pulled me closer to you and wiped my lip
with back of one sugar-stained hand

You said:

I didn't mean to burn you at the end
like you do to your cigarettes on this porch,
I was trying to inhale,
but you were made of smoke

I could never put my finger on you,
but you're underneath my nails
the ash,
I smell you on the wind every time I breathe

It all makes sense to me
we've lived right down the street from each other
this whole time
and I've been sending smoke signals
out into the city begging you to see me
burning down—
one word stories of what it's like to tear twigs
from your own branches
to keep the signal fire lighting my remaining shape
into the sky
you may be out of sight now, we don't talk
about things like that anymore

in this dream you become a flower
in the least poetic way,
rooted into my dirty cheeks
your petals fresh packets of Kool-Aid

I woke from it in a pain
that was so far beyond words
it felt like the closest thing
to the truth I have ever known
for three weeks that feeling stayed
and every day I came home from work knowing
I haven't burned enough yet to be seen

a bad taste

bitterness,
you were my old best friend
we read comics together
lamenting that the size of our imaginations
bore no weight on uneven scales

we called it strength,
when we resorted to resentment—
soured down to roots until
the soil flaked and caused a drought

you always held some words for me
to throw at other people
you became the sound stuck in my mouth
I only wanted to get out

I am trying
to spit out the bitter
but I'm just so used
to the taste

something wicked this way comes

when its cloud finally arrives to rain
I will edit this poem,
roll it taught
slide it into a bullet casing
watch the end flare up,
the ink mix with gun powder,
the words fold
under the falling hammer,
it will ignite
into a firework,
just like a poem is
meant to be

its spray will paint police blockades, riot masks
its lineation will conjure a face
we couldn't hold long enough to be taken seriously,
an idea that can not be stricken down
or legislated away,
the sentiment that we are larger
than the way we die

a thread

there is a thread running through america

between ground beef and hamburger buns
around bowls of macaroni salad and lakes
lined with houses rich people own
and still rent to ghosts of the middle class

woven into Stars and Stripes, like
a wick leading to fireworks on the 4th of July
it's the hair in your slice of apple pie
sewn into smallpox blankets
handed out at football games

a thread that leads to an end tied around
the trigger of a gun
aimed directly at
ourselves

periods like bullet holes

bought a notebook on the day
another gunman opened fire in San Bernardino, California
It called to me from the shelf of a discount store
In the car, the radio had mentioned an active shooter
and those wavelengths were still playing off the
insides of my head
their bend, a twist, to not let me forget
It called to me like the voices of those
whose chapter closed
the displacement of so many breaths never taken
pushed air through it
like a closing page

And I picked it up and felt the black grip,
ran my fingers in the golden type face
I hoped I could fill the pages
with descriptions of things I thought were beautiful
and broken, and scarred, and twisted
in just the right way
before a gunman opens fire here

vaudeville

I have cleaned up well
there is a show tonight

my rows of seats ready, spread
so that everyone gets a view

the floors are clean
no where to get stuck when they file in

and everyone with a ticket gets a seat
my silver screen shows demons defeated

by heroes splashed in empty computer graphics
just to make sure we know that heroes aren't real

we have reached the future —
and tonight, there is a man coming
for his fifteen minutes of fame

bringing songs with melodies made of click-clack's
baring all the skin we keep in safe spaces

he has been instructed in houses like mine
living rooms in america filled
with more guns than people

more trigger pulls than words

he is coming with guns he bought online
just like his ticket to the show

LOST

LOST looks like 3:18 am on the cable box
with Donald Trump flailing
his meat hooks everywhere
It looks like Facebook comments that mock people
whose lives just got a lot harder—
It looks like apathy

LOST smells like the inside of an empty PBR can
the flowers at a funeral you didn't expect to be at
LOST smells like a perfume you can't forget,
but it's been so long since
that you have for a while

LOST sounds like the ringing phone
you're too afraid to answer
voicemails from your Grandmother
you can't bring yourself to delete
LOST sounds like church bells
signaling you to the last place
there's anything to find
LOST sounds like believing
you can be found anyway

LOST tastes like cigarettes after a bad bender
the hangover making last night crawl
back up your throat
it tastes like teeth you forgot to brush,
food you didn't buy
LOST tastes like blood

LOST feels like an empty room full of people
your voice tearing in an echo chamber
that keeps you screaming at yourself
LOST feels like a boat
out on the water
whose motor just died

LOST feels alone
LOST feels like freedom

to see them weightless

I still invite
my dead friends
to Facebook events
like a keyboard séance

I would love to see them weightless—
come in through the venue door
with a hand in the air
strength to carry the bags under their eyes

after the show, we'd slap each others backs
to the beat of the old days
reminisce until we astral projected
back to the old haunts

and when they'd ask:
how ya been, Ben?
I wouldn't answer, only say
better now that you're here
I was scared for a while
you'd become a period
at the end of one of my sentences.

in life, my dead friends
were the heaviest people I knew
modern day Marley's
forging links to chains they carried
no one else saw

people called it costume jewelry
as if a string of needles and displacement
were fake pearls to adorn a neckline

my living friend Meg
is a white water rafting instructor
who writes poetry that helps me
navigate the rough patches
of the bends in my heart

in Philadelphia we saw
a grounded hot air balloon,
she mentions the experience of a basket floating
down to hold hands with her in the river
and all I can think of are the sticks
Justin picked out of Caz creek
when he started making those Carcosa sculptures

you know, True Detective?
you know, going crazy?
you know, the kind of thing a friend would notice
and hold against themselves
when they don't

when he joked with me that he got pulled over
with his new girlfriend and an old accomplice
and the old friend got in trouble
for the scale under his seat
the powder that was on it—
the rubber bands and balloons in the ashtray
I should have...

When my living friend Meg
tells me about hot air balloons
all I can think of is how little
I want to die on one—
either from the fire of the burner,
or jumping from the basket
the air being pulled from my lungs either way

she says:
did you hear about that guy at Letchworth?

She says:
when you're wrangling hot air balloons
and one gets loose
you're supposed to let go of the cord

if you don't it'll carry you up—
and this guy didn't let go
until he was a hundred feet in the air

it has been two years since
they found the only hot air balloon wrangler
I have ever known, face down
on the desk where he did his best work
as if one had finally gotten loose
and his fingers were so wrapped around the cord
he didn't have time to untie the knots

the shock of being unable to let go
of carrying us so far into the sky
chasing the things that elevate us
that by the time we're a hundred feet up
we just want to be part of the view below

the memory of my dead friend
is like a bundle of birthday balloons in my hand
each ribbon breaking from my wrist
as I watch another year pass

I can feel the cord between my hands
chaffing against my palms, knowing
that it's finally time
to let go

my friends

my friends,
are lit wicks
with fuses leading to boxes labeled
'tragedy'
we all went to the same summer camp
dipped our toes in death's myth-pool young
became Thestrals and couldn't stop
seeing the truth everywhere

my friends,
are night brawlers
and bare knuckle boxers
white tape across their noses
from the fist fights with themselves
this is part of why I like them—
they're some of the only people I know
that practice accountability
introspection sharp as broken mirror shards

my friends,
siphon comfort from whiskey bottles
will spend their last dollar
to make a moment last
I don't think my friends have ever thought
about what that will leave them at forty
I know I haven't

my friends,
are astronauts
pen strokes constructing galaxies due for exploration

challengers catching fire—
leaving stories in their smoke trails

my friends,
                    are black holes
appearing dangerous and unapproachable
really singularities trying to pull the universe close
while being particularly bad at letting go of things

my friends,
                    stare into the abyss and smile—
not because they're brave,
but because they studied Nietzsche
ten years ago
and life is clearly more nuanced than that
plus quantum foam is more interesting

my friends,
                    don't give themselves enough credit
they wouldn't be used to it if they started to
throw it up like a starving man given caviar—
this comes with wearing the rust belt

my friends,
                    are used to the let down
of trains running late,
regardless of politician's promises
of making a career in poverty
no matter how much they master their calling

my friends,
                    are carpenters

flush with enough claptrap and nails
to build homes
so common sense has a place to rest its head
they keep hammers handy
to seal off the storm cellar
important, now that the winds have begun to change
they create storage shelters for the word hoarders
engineer Story Ark's against the rising tide

pull your finger from the plug

didn't know what to expect
blank faces and loaded glances
oh—this is the poetry guy
can't wait for this to be over

just finished a poem at tapestry charter school—
three hundred kids clapping
and I am disappointed in myself
was only an old man yelling at them
assumed they missed the point

the room is dark
hear someone suck in air through their nose
to hold back tears

the gymnasium clears out, but there's one kid
he's as tall as me and maybe sixteen
he comes up to me with tears in his eyes
says: *thank you*

late at night I think of the people I've talked to—
wonder if I've ever managed to deconstruct a wall
brick by brick
or if these bloody knuckles I carry daily
are just a sign walls can't be brought down

we walk through the charter school halls—
he tells me he wanted to kill himself,
but he's doing better now
his girlfriend helps,

I give him my card.
when he sends a message on instagram
I don't respond

it's the summer and I'm teaching poetry to kids
they tell me it's boring
envy them and wonder
what it's like to find someone's suicide note uninteresting

six months pass before I message him back
apologize for being busy
and think of empty nights I've spent since
drunk in front of a computer screen
convincing other people I'm a writer

why do we ignore the ones most like ourselves?

they always thank me for coming—
never sure what to say when they tell me it helped
glad they have seen what cracks in the dam look like
hope they have learned
how to pull their finger from the plug

he never messages me back
I think about that a lot

because it's funny, isn't it?

You come in through the front door and the handle hits the wall so hard it breaks through and pieces of wall pour out like sand. I barely even notice because the sunlight is across your cheek in this way that makes me think of porcelain dolls my Aunt had lined on the armoire of her guest bedroom.

Staying at my Aunt's was a big deal, you know? She was one of those people that God's green thumb spent a little extra time on. She let me pick my own cereal and made me chocolate chip pancakes shaped like Mickey Mouse's head just 'cause. She was one of those places where the world felt like it could be good. Just out and out good. For no other reason than that it should be.

This one time, when I still believed in God, I said I thought the only way there'd be a hostile alien invasion is if He was testing us. It was the summer Independence Day came out and I remembered swelling with pride when Will Smith punched that alien in the head and said: *Welcome to Earth!*

She listened to me intently, despite none of it making sense and said, "The way things are now I'm not sure we wouldn't deserve it." I still don't know what she meant by that.

Behind you, through the front door, the world's on fire, but inside the A/C is still working. I can hear the flow of it coming from the vents and dancing on my skin. It still feels normal inside and here you are comin' through the front door.

The necklace you got that summer when we went to Cedar Point is around your neck, just some twine and a few stupid beads. You always wore it, though because you got it right after I finally rode a rollercoaster.

It seems like another life now. But we were twenty-three and I was still afraid of everything. You said if you're afraid of something you have to square up with it because almost nothing is as bad as it seems.

But your cheek isn't porcelain, and it's not a trick of the light.

We loved staying at my Aunt's house 'cause that's where the world was always good, you know?

At Cedar Point I rode the Dragster and the only thing as scary as that feeling in my chest when I couldn't pull my head from the seat was when I asked you to marry me.

You're coming through the door and I put my arms out to catch you at about the same time I realize the red on your mouth isn't lipstick. Why would it be? You have your gym clothes on. The world's on fire behind you.

But those dolls. They had eyes and they'd watch you when you slept. They always had this look. I had bad dreams about them sometimes when I'd think I woke up and one of them would be right next to me and whisper in my ear: Maybe you deserve it.

After I got off the ride you hugged me from behind and said: See, it isn't so bad, right? And it wasn't so bad with you there. Nothing really was.

Your cheekbone is as beautiful as I expected it would be. The world and our front lawn are on fire.

When I got older my Aunt moved into my Grandmother's house after she died. She put the porcelain dolls on an old China cabinet in the basement. I could never remember what felt so scary about them.

I knew pretty soon after we got off the Dragster that I was going to ask you to marry me.

You crash into me so hard we go tumbling. You land on top of me and I lose my air when I hit the ground. As soon as I get it back, the fire's at the front door, and I'm laughing.

Because it's funny, isn't it?

resurgence

come up
rise, like
a city always
up, but never
quite there yet
share in the
loganberry wit
the silly puns
off names and
place we still
see only as
a punchline

7 a.m. in buffalo

it's 7 a.m.
and the radio is banging away about
how the Bills are awful—
I have this feeling that if I close my eyes
and let go of the wheel
I'd end up crashed into something that someone
would have taken a picture of
and hashtagged
#thatssobuffalo

the flames would eat up the. rust
on the side of my car
and in my dying moments
I'd think about some weird metaphor
for the steel industry
going out on some narrative
my location has always bolted me to

this all feels normal
I'm very used to this at 7 a.m.

Jack Eichel has just busted his leg
years of being bad on purpose
just to finally see some glimmer of hope
and it goes out like a capped candle
second chances skating on icy rinks
that leave it almost impossible to stand up

it makes you wonder if second chances are real

or if they don't just shove you out there
to see what you look like scrambling

#thatssobuffalo

I come around the curve to the 290
and right before it splits
to take me away from Tonawanda
I see these balloons on the roadside—
they're dipping their heads on the shoulder
drifting up away to
let their ribbons come to rest
among the uncut grass—
they're the kind I used to sell
to flustered single mothers at Dollar General
shining silver,
the material like some star ship
beneath my fingertips

and in that short period of time
the span that coffee will wash away
when sleep still dances on your eyelids
when you ask yourself what the fuck you are doing
doing what you're doing
without ever asking yourself
why you're doing it

when you wonder if this is all it is
the same construction zones
where you can't go over 45 mph
for 6 months at a time
or wide right,

or Jack Eichel busting his fucking leg
the day before the season starts

in that time I start to ask myself if we aren't all just
balloons floating on the roadside
being pushed around
by whatever we happen to be surrounded by
put there as placeholders for things that could have
had a choice
memorials deflating
our lives—
memorials made of air

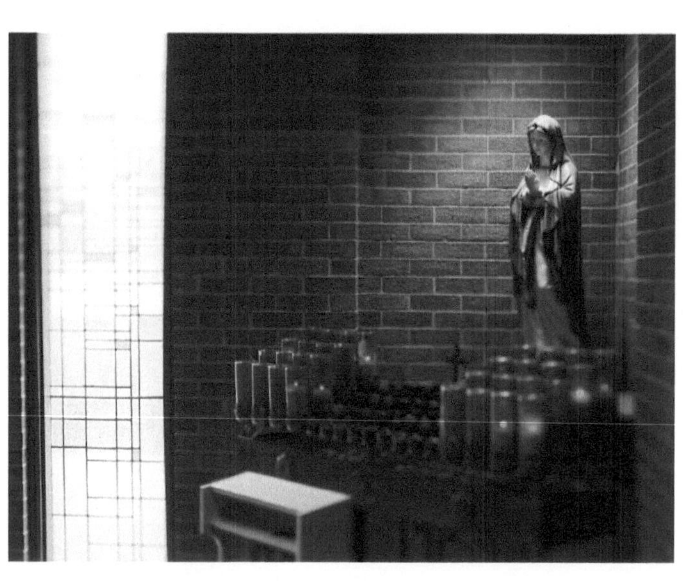

Those Who Pray To Fire

the last time I was really happy, Emilio Estevez was coaching peewee hockey

yesterday, while I was on my
usual midnight pilgrimage,
walking down Richmond Ave.
and doing my best Steve McQueen
I heard the quacking of ducks.

I looked all around and didn't see anything—
and yet, the quacking persisted.
I assumed there was a springtime V
in the sky I didn't see.

it sounded like a resurrection symphony
and as I lit up a cigarette, I thought of Dan McKeon
and his poem about ducks, depression,
and rigor mortis burritos.

it brought a smile to my face
knowing there's so much interesting writing
happening in Buffalo.
it brought a smile to my face knowing that
somewhere in the city
there was a gang of heartbroken ducks
burning their antidepressants
and carjacking Lloyd Taco Trucks.
I imagined them driving into the night
toward the west coast,
gorging themselves on shells and salsa
while using the grease to write micropoems
in the window frost about how life
can and will be better.

cock cousins disappearing in the rust belt when there's no one else left to fuck

last night an ex slapped me hard across the face
we were at a bar and I was blacked out
a friend told me about it in the morning
apparently I asked for another
that's the kind of lover I am
I'm also a high-functioning alcoholic
at least I don't have delirium tremens

I think that's the problem with america
it has stopped drinking
and it's experiencing severe alcohol
withdrawal symptoms all that shaking
confusion and hallucinations
it's scary out there
it's like what Oscar Wilde said

They've promised that dreams can come true
But forgot to mention that nightmares are dreams, too

my worst nightmare is a bunch of my ex-lovers
crowdfunding a strip club to mock me
where they showcase their squiggles
of bones at my expense
where some high-profile DJ in a star-studded booth
spins records of my greatest drunk voicemails,
when I'm crying like a whale
with a bomb in its mouth,
blubbering about my failures
how I miss you,

how I'm a fuck-up, how I drink too much,
how I can't stop, how I'll never stop,
oh the first-world humanity...

my worst nightmare is all my ex-lovers
taking off their skins
while dancing to the rhythm of my lowest moments
and all I can do is sit and watch
and make testosterone smoothies out of rocks,
car parts and glass
cause I need to toughen up,
cause I think I'm still in love
with every shipwreck in the Great Lakes
and that means I gotta get ice crystals in my blood
and freeze over
like the greatest men in american history
hopeless nautical robots drowning their sorrows
in drink and sex

who am I kidding?
my worst nightmare is that I'm at my best when
I'm hopeless and tasty
like the sushi you pluck from dead men's eyes
I'm afraid I may become a fuck boy
my worst nightmare is that my future lovers
are at their best when words pour out their mouths
like the bulimia of fireflies
I'm afraid they'll burn me alive
as I disappear into the Bermuda Triangle
of who's fucking who
everyone wearing masks and saving face

sometimes it's easier to pretend that you don't care
that's how you survive without losing your mind

not giving a fuck
that's what it's all about, really

impress your friends and amaze yourself
plus, ladies love guys that don't give a fuck
we're all lonely and missing something
but you can't cuddle with a zombie

your melancholy is straight out of an Edith Piaf song

in Buffalo the love is cheap
a pretty girl wondering what to do
with the dizziness
there's only so much whiskey I can drink
in hopes that things will get interesting
or real to the touch

when you black out
your brain loses its ability to form memories
but your heart gains the ability to spit passion
in all directions
like a cobra projecting venom from its fangs
when defending itself
I'll take that trade-off every time

and yet there are nights I want to remember
nights I want to kiss you in the glow
of the Buffalo State Hospital
where the phantoms of psychosis are held down
by the giants of memory
where birds of feelings
are always crashing into invisible windows
and their little bodies Hindenburg out of the sky
until the ground is littered with what appears to be
dry, dead leaves

sometimes things fall apart
so that better things can fall together

sometimes it's the simplest fucking thing
that makes me happy

watching you dance in the rain
while I conjure the ghost of Edith Piaf
with a smartphone Ouija board

gathering together dead body parts to assemble the next president of the united states

it's summer here so frostbitten crust punks
are touching themselves in the amber glow
of backyard bonfires on Buffalo's lower west side.
they're trying to warm up
to the idea that Bernie Sanders will not be
the next president of the united states.
I can hear them weeping and moaning
as I walk up Delavan thinking about my on-again
off-again girlfriend.
sometimes I dream
that I'm Frankenstein
she's my bandage-wrapped bride
and we're both composed of dead body parts
from all the people who've screwed us over.
I over-romanticize everything, but it's so important
to be connected to something larger than yourself.
even in this sea of sadness,
choose your battles wisely
and hang on tight.
tonight, I will make love to my on-again
off-again girlfriend on a bed of Bernie Sanders
for President yard signs and afterwards, we'll dream
of better things. it'll be like necrophilia
and when we wake up, there'll be snow
on the ground
and all this will be lost.

we're living in closets full of snow

it's like drilling for oil, Sam tells me
he's shoveling snow
and still wearing those therapy pajamas
with the bottom part of the pants cut
it's bitter cold out here
like something out of Game of Thrones
but Sam likes getting frostbite
says it makes him feel alive
that the freezing of body tissues
reminds him that he still has a body
and that's all you can really ask for these days
the backyard is full of glow-in-the-dark junk
a lawn sprinkler douses us in bare-knuckled bourbon
and bruises my spirit
but not Sam's
he has shoveled three times so far tonight
convinced that there are Vitamin D supplements
buried under the snow
he tells me that happiness flashes suddenly
and is gone
like how when you fall asleep
in the Rust Belt and there's no snow
but then you wake up
and see that some blizzard painted the ground
with its tears while you were dreaming
and Sam dreams a lot
like he's Edgar Cayce or something,
a lot of times he dreams of this small town graveyard
full of television sets
and they're all tuned in to a live coverage
of dead men's stag parties

he tells me that testosterone is leaving this land
but that might be a good thing
he yells at me for always falling in love
with the same kind of girl
the kind that feels the urge
to jump off a bridge all the time
the kind that will probably get postpartum depression
I tell him he's being sexist
and Sam tells me I'm probably right
sometimes Sam shovels
even when there isn't any snow
one day I'll cut bathtubs out of his eyes
and soak in his speakeasies of sadness
and together we'll hold hands and jump off a bridge

we might be fuck-ups
but at least we're not douchebags

and that's pretty important,
to still give a shit
to still think there's happiness
out there somewhere

picking fruit off the sick future

Megan dropped her leftover poutine
cause she suddenly turned around
like she felt the touch of a ghost
but it was just the smell of lilacs from a nearby bush
she told me lilacs remind her of the south
of growing up as a military brat
of these gilded manors as big as the sun
ladies who would apply lipstick to the dirt
to make it pretty

I looked her straight in her stoned eyes
and told her we're always on our hands and knees
always trying to glamorize the world beneath our feet
that's how you make it in america these days
by brainwashing the dead
we keep chained down in our basements
until they're perfect slaves
picking fruit off the sick future

I was stoned too
but it felt like the right thing to say

america is going crazy these days
and sometimes the only antidote
is to go crazy, too
and who cares if it's like 3 a.m.
and you have work before sunrise
and you feel like your world is falling apart
that all your friends are either brain-gone
or so restless

they're always on paralysis treadmills
and hoping for the worst

we don't know healthy from unhealthy anymore

suddenly we noticed a trail of poutine gravy
on the sidewalk melting
in the Rust Belt moonlight
like that Gestapo agent's face in
Raiders of the Lost Ark
a reminder that you can't stare into the eyes
of something bigger than yourself
Megan didn't care though
she stepped over all that gook
and plucked a lilac from the bush
I lit a cigarette and tried to take it all in

it was tough not to think of heavenly fire
that something bigger than us still burns inside us
and it doesn't have to be large
or so intense it burns holes in time
it could just mean you're sharing secondhand smoke
with someone who understands you
and maybe that's what's most important about
living in crazy times
remembering the little things that make us human

me and Megan walked around
the whole city that night
we were careful not to check our phones
worried we'd be reminded of all our dying friends
or all our ex-lovers
masturbating to the mistakes we've made

we also didn't want to be screamed at
by a nation losing its mind

a nation that performs lobotomies
on museums and art galleries
just so we'll forget where we come from
just so we'll forget the beauty that's out there
a nation that attaches wings to the backs of its devils
so they can soar above the skyline
like chemtrails feeding us amnesia

the thing is,
sometimes I think we've forgotten how to feel
when the memory rushing in hits our hearts
and our emotional cords close suddenly
and we're left with big hieroglyphic hiccups
strange uncontrollable noises we don't understand
like translating from a language we don't know
I guess we must do whatever it takes
to get us to remember
but it's not for everyone

that night me and Megan walked
over hills and everywhere
and when the atmosphere got too lobotomized
she smelled the lilac like it was a drug
rocketing memory to her brain
when the atmosphere got too lobotomized
I just lit up another cigarette
and tried to forget who I was

memory has never looked good on me anyway
but it looks good on her

when the sun came up
we were in front of her place

we hugged
and that was it

afterwards I went back
to that trail of melting gravy

and followed it
until I got lost
and never looked back

I still have a long way to go

the green breast of the New World is in Allentown

tonight I was restless and went walking,
looking for F. Scott Fitzgerald's childhood home,
because he lived on Irving Place as a boy
and because I wanted to talk to his memory
about the fresh, green breast of the new world.

I found the place and stared at it for a while.

after about two cigarettes,
I grew even more restless
and decided to build a boat out of other men's eyes.
I sailed across an ocean looking for things
that only I could see.

there was nothing but driftwood
and the faint sounds of jazz

emanating from underground galaxies.
I sat and listened until my restlessness
found a home in my hand.

vomiting into a toilet is democracy in action

god is feeding dust storms to all his little animals
most of us are hooting and hollering
in three-second spurts
a group of jack-in-the-box cheerleaders
on our last springs
cause Sam's standing atop
the walnut wood coffee table
looking like a strung out Statue of Liberty
and declaring, give me your tired, your poor,
your huddled masses,
yearning to let go and soar,
yearning for a better lifestyle...
some party-goers get a little crazy
and tear the city apart
the decaying industrial factories along the waterfront
go up in flames
later in the night Sam gets to the point
of being so upset
that he's throwing up like a baby
and I rub his back like a good friend
I'm also holding his Salvation Army sports coat
close to my heart
so that it doesn't get covered in vomit
and I have to laugh
cause all I see when I look at him
is a sweaty Statue of Liberty
hunched over the Atlantic
and emptying out all our dreams
like an oil tanker with slit wrists
coming to terms with its own crudeness

and when he's done puking I help him up
and we go outside for some air
zombie chauffeurs in fedoras
are shuffling our friends into stretch limos
and we know we'll never see them again…
if we could, we would jump
into puddles of american tears
and splash them to the sky
like dynamite breaking down a door…
maybe god would hear us then

a beach party for animals that have gone extinct

she tried to stab me with a vibrator
I was in the process of moving out
I got the hell out of there
but before leaving I took one of her bottles
of Fireball cinnamon whisky
I don't even like Fireball
but I couldn't resist the poetry of the moment
a relationship was over and done with
extinct, as if it was hit by the asteroid
that killed the dinosaurs
in other words, the dinosaurs drank too much fire
I was hoping the whiskey would do the same to me
I did really love her
so I drank the entire bottle
and wandered around the city
I must've blacked out
because when I came to
I was on a pretty beach somewhere
which was strange
because there are no pretty beaches
where I come from
I was at a beach party for animals
that have gone extinct
there were neanderthal djs
spinning fossil records
on a couple of x-ray turntables
I was grinding up against a wooly mammoth
and tickling its ivory keys
it was the hottest thing I've ever done

the music of extinction
gets the dance floor moving
I got into a fight with a saber-toothed tiger
and won
I pulled out its teeth
with rusted pliers and cried afterwards
the big angry cat was so beautiful
when the sun started to come up
a bunch of dodo birds took flight
and they were holding tiny vibrators
in their weird-looking beaks
I watched them fly over the water
where they dropped the vibrators
like they were sad sex bombs
it was the most amazing thing
I've ever seen, not to mention
that dodo birds lost the ability to fly
while they were still alive
so I guess that means
it takes a little bit of extinction
for us to regain the best parts of ourselves
it filled me with optimism
watching those dumb birds fly
watching those vibrators drown
in the dirty water
so I guess that means
we shouldn't focus so much
on pleasuring ourselves
because if we do
we'll just end up drowning alone
that maybe we should focus
on pleasuring the dead things
that are all around us

that maybe we should make sense
of extinction and hope for the best
when the sun did finally come up
I was walking to a café
so I could eat an overpriced bagel
and drink lukewarm coffee
and hopefully plan for the rest of my life

self-destructive people have a leg up on life

leaving for work today,
I had to brush snow off my car.
typical.

there was this woman across the street
brushing the snow off her car.
again, typical.

however, suddenly I heard her scraping ice
and I thought, there's no ice on my car.

then I coughed and spit into the street
and it made sense
since I got home, like, two hours ago.
I'd been out.
my car never had the time
to dress up in ice.
see?
stay out late chasing love,
make a game of strip mining your carcass
and maybe the mornings
won't be so brutal.

maybe you won't be so cold.

there's no christmas in the afterlife

on the corner of Summer and Elmwood,
a taxicab driver waves me over,
because he needs a light.
I ask him how he's doing.
he tells me he's trying to make some money,
so he can be Santa for his kids.

how sad
being a taxicab driver in Buffalo,
in a city where we all drive drunk,
where we don't believe in death,
in being ferried by a boatman
across a river of memories.

Santa Claus won't be coming this year.

the rise and fall of the Canalside christmas tree

part one

it's december third
and I'm walking along the water at Canalside
toward the big christmas tree
near First Niagara Center.

not really big—
this is Buffalo after all—
so much as mangled, uneven, languishing
like that tree in A Charlie Brown Christmas.

tonight is the lighting ceremony
and everyone seems ready
and delighted about it,
but I'm not,
because I read the news today,

like that Beatles song,
and I read that hundreds of babies
are expected to go through withdrawal this year
as the opioid epidemic continues in Erie County,

babies who can't self sooth,
with rub marks on their faces,
their knees, and their elbows
from trying to comfort themselves—
and then raging—
against the linen.
a lot of mothers are in fear.

so, yeah,
the christmas tree looks like a syringe
aimed heavenwards
and I know that when the lights get turned on,
the sky will go numb
and no fat messiah will come

and up in the sky youthful clouds will overdose
and spit out smelly snow
and all the old clouds will roll around
in the mess and cry about
what could've been

and down here on the ground,
all the hourglasses will be body bagged in frostbite
and me and everyone I know
will be enthroned in used tissues
making origami spirit animals
out of the things that make us sick

and deep down,
we're hoping it's true that times of tragedy
reveal true leadership,
that when all is said and done,
we'll climb to the sky
and resurrect all the dead clouds

then we'll carry them on our backs
until we're in a different sky
looking down on a different earth,
a different city,
and all those youthful clouds
that had so much potential

will rain out their regrets
and snow out their silences
and this Different Earth will be flooded
with flowers that understand pain and failure.

when the christmas tree bursts into fake flames,
I'm sitting on a bench across from the Tim Hortons
chain smoking strokes and getting dizzy.

suddenly
I'm hit by sadness and now I'm getting desperate,
so I grab my iPhone, go on YouTube and look up
christmas commercials from the 80's—
I want to miss my childhood again.

I want my faith restored,
to believe in a gentler form of capitalism,
for Nintendos of hot chocolate to melt
the heroin in my heart
until my power's back on
and I can leave the house again
without the world always going to shit.

I want to play outside
and shove my face into buffets of the freshest snow,
eat a world that isn't getting warmer.
I want to have drinks with polar bears
in ice bars at the edge of the universe.
I don't want kids to die.
I just want the world to be a better place.

the anger is rising though
and there's no telling where it will end.

drug dependent babies everywhere
will burst out of their prenatal coffins
like little Nosferatus
or like betrayed toys on christmas morning
breaking out of their boxes just to scream at us,

to tell us that playtime's over,
that it's time to get real,
like that show on MTV
but it's not like the old days anymore.
so I guess all of us gotta get bulimic
about our nostalgia
and purge it from our systems.

we look fat and disgusting
clinging to what we do,
while ignoring the world around us,
and it's like we wear nostalgia around our necks
like nooses

and when there's always a noose around your neck,
it's always that much easier for the world
to hang you out to dry.
we must be stronger—
now, more than ever.
now I want a drink.

I don't know,
maybe I'm jealous of drug dependent babies,

that they came into this world gripping addiction
while me and everyone I know
are desperate to get it.

now I'm staring at all the families circling
around the big christmas tree

singing slaver songs and snuffing out reality.
I finish my cigarette and head to Panorama
on Seven nearby
where Dale feeds me Old Fashioneds
until I'm good and drunk

and feeling old fashioned myself
like a medieval town crier.

now I'm ready to bawl my eyes out
with any stranger ready to play.
as I exit the bar,
I notice the big christmas tree is still all lit up

and the light is so blinding and scary
like something out of Genesis.
I imagine me and everyone I know
being swallowed up by its flames.
I know what I must do:
I walk up to the big christmas tree and undo my fly.

I begin to piss all over it
hoping it will put out all those little flames.
I put everything I have into the piss—
all my anger, nostalgia, sadness,
hope for the future—
but the big christmas tree, it just keeps burning,
because no matter how much piss you have in you,
you can't put out a fake fire.

now I'm dejected,
aware of all the failure inside me,
so I fall to my knees
and light up yet another cigarette,
because cancer seems like a real good idea now

and suddenly,
I hear the cries of babies all around me—
roaring out of the distance,
roaring from across the water—
and then I see them, crawling toward me,
all the drug dependent babies.
they're coming for us all,
for revenge.

I begin to crawl toward them too,
hoping we can meet in the middle,
but deep down,
I know that's not enough—
now, more than ever.
I will let them kill me
and there will be a smile on my cold, dead face

when they dump my old fashioned body
into the water. there will be
an even bigger smile on my cold, dead face
when my ghost listens to them conquer the city
and then the world.

part two

yesterday
I watched men
wearing neon beanies
take down the christmas tree
at Canalside.

I was chain smoking
and impressed
with their surgical precision.

their chainsaws were singing
like drunk actors
at karaoke.

I was taken aback by the fact
that no one else was watching.
it made me angry,
because it seems so many of us
just half-ass our way through life.

during the lighting ceremony,
there were families everywhere.

where was everyone
when the tree was cut
to pieces like a steak?

it's important to experience
both a rise and fall.
one must first self-destruct
to truly appreciate a rebirth –

and these days,
when everything around us
is being cut to pieces,
I think it's important
for us to throw
our whole bodies
into the american surgery.

we can't just pay attention
when things are pretty;

we must get our hands angry
and dirty.

all of our fists,
including our hearts,
must rise up in protest.

bring on the chainsaws.

it is our responsibility to reassemble
and be as strong
as we possibly can.

so it turns out I'm an asshole who has a cold sore fetish

saturday morning in Western New York:

the cashier at Tim Hortons has a sore
on her lower lip.
I assume the worst.
while ordering an extra-large coffee,
I stare at it
like some 3D painting –
really focusing my eyes, y'know,
in hopes of seeing the bigger picture.
maybe it's a passion bump, I think,
a sexualized icicle frozen over time.
too many winters, I think.
suddenly the sore starts growing
and opens up its bloom for me, beckoning me.
I walk right in and think,
is this how the Puritans felt
when they hopped off the boat
and stepped onto america's shore for the first time?
when that star-spangled wilderness
hugged them for the first time?

the land of opportunity, I think.

anyway, after walking around for a bit,
I find myself in a garden
where all the flowers have gramophones for faces

and when they sing,
it sounds scratchy…but perfect,
because we all have an itch
we can't reach.
I sit and listen closely,
because there's so much of me I can't reach.
when I come to,
I'm handing the cashier some money.
her sore looks like a harvest moon and it's beautiful,
a satellite that transforms gas station parking lots
into cornfields of astronomy.

afterwards,
while sitting in my car,
all I keep thinking about
is how much of an asshole I am.

even when we're at our worst we're still cut from the same cloth

in the beginning your life
was a special kind of speed boat
racing across waves of Morse code
over a seafloor littered with dead languages.
you were never afraid of getting lost
in translation, because
you were confident that love
and sometimes passion
shoves life back into
unfamiliar bones,
that although history is one big closet
that billions of skeletons call home,
all it takes is the strength
of your heart to fling open
the door to emancipate the pain
and set the world free.

but that was a long time ago,
when your overconfidence
overflowed in abundance outta you,
now look at you.
tonight you put too much water
in the pot when making pasta,
because you were distracted,
lonely and needing pasta,
because pasta suggests there's a foundation
of family in your life,
or so you think

prolly because of the whole
Italian thing.
it's especially sad when you crush
up your antidepressants
and sprinkle them like parmesan cheese
over the cheap noodles.
it's even sadder when you're eating it
while watching *Eternal Sunshine of the Spotless Mind*
for, like, the millionth time,
because the mind's so monstrous
and you understand that forced amnesia
is sometimes the best option
and anyway, Kate Winslet's so adorable,
working at Barnes & Noble
where you worked at for six years.
she's so cute
you want to flagellate yourself
because she's a manic pixie
dream girl and you pride yourself
on never objectifying anyone
and you feel like a hypocrite,
but goddamn, all those colors in her hair!
you're always anxious thinking
you're not living your life
to the fullest looking
for your own peace of mind.

as you finish the rest of your
antidepressant alfredo,
you make quips to all of your imaginary friends
about how *Eternal Sunshine of the Spotless Mind*
is from an Alexander Pope poem,
that maybe what you need

more than anything is
to go on a vision quest inside the cataracts
of cracked-out angels,
but none of your friends – real
or imaginary – ever listen
to your cries for help.

things, it seems, never quite go according to plan.
there was a time, maybe long ago,
when you and everyone around you
understood each other's Morse code.
now look at you all,
scratching at deafness hoping
to erase the itch of words gone unsaid.
blessed are the forgetful.
you look at a baby, and it's so pure
and so free and so clean – and adults are, like,
this mess
of sadness,

so you walk the streets at night
weeping for millions of mouthless streetlights,
because deep down
you know how thirsty they must be.
struggling against the persistent darkness,
losing too much
of themselves in the war
for shine.

you imagine they're desperate to drink
themselves to death,
especially when the daylight takes all the credit
for holding the city's sanity together.
these are nights you take your lumbering body

and scale up streetlights on Richmond Ave.
and punch their faces open to create mouths,
then you pour in whatever liquor you swiped
from your ex's apartment – usually gin
and you don't care much for gin.
whiskey's your lover,
because you imagine it's what god's piss tastes like,
that when he created the oceans,
it's because he broke the seal.

then you imagine that the ocean floor
is just one giant whiskey dick.
sad,
but when it gets going...
those tsunamis of rage
libidos more like shipwrecks
than proof of procreation,
silent dinners with lying lovers
suddenly erupting over
the breaking of tectonic plates,
everything shifting when you're not ready,

you're not ready to move on.
you're never ready to move on.

oh, these are nights you water board streetlights
with cheap gin
in hopes they start dancing,
that they start feeling good about themselves,
that they finally kick the darkness.
sometimes you try to transform yourself
into a flickering streetlight by rooting
your feet into the ground
and lighting your hair on fire

until you're dazed and contused
and the darkness feels safe again,
until we're all beautiful birds
perched on podiums of hope
and preaching that we should never abandon
each other when we're at our worst.

you tell yourself
that you should be breaking the chains
not falling into the statistics.
making it up from poverty.
fighting over the smallest words.
because there's the chance you might die
in a car crash
and there's still so much love left
to thrust, a thievery sandwiched between ear
and shoulder, when the knot
in your brain bursts and a million thoughts
build you a skyscraper of what you want
from the ground up –
so give it another go, because there's beauty
in getting another chance to fuck it all up again.
everything happening to you
right here, right now
is proof that destiny is making
the night sky go all leprosy
and the moon is shitting out binoculars
for your eyes to get another go
at finding silver linings.

there is already so much light
that you carry in your hands,
that you should carry it toward the darkness

on the other side of us all.

maybe if you try to be the best person
you can possibly be,
then maybe your bones won't limp
to the finish line
like jellyfish tailgating outside of funeral homes.

you're better than this.
you're better than walking alongside railroad tracks
from cerebellum to crotch hoping
all the poltergeists in your life
will stop pussyfooting around and possess you
completely, so that you'll derail
into rock bottom, so that by morning,
you'll be gone.

the end...now don't erase this
from your memory.
look at you,
your eyes ablaze, playing spin
the telescope with speakeasy astronomers.
everything is
going to be
okay.

elegy for 2016 and maybe the death of america

New Year's Eve
and the man on the car radio tells me,
good news:
you might not be fat;
you might just be bloated.

dead bodies are often bloated,
so it seems that being dead
is better than being fat.
I did eat, like,
hundreds of pierogis last night.
I also slept for ten hours.
if anything, I'm bloated on dreams
and if that makes me dead or dying,
I'm okay with it.

I go get a peppermint mocha
before heading to work
and as I'm smoking
in front of Starbucks on Elmwood,
a wave of optimistic nausea hits me:
despite us living in an age of dead princesses,
we still have the power to be like royalty.
despite us living in an age
when all our favorite musicians
are washing up on beaches,
we still have the power
to walk along shores
and find severed vocal cords

like seashells
buried in the sand.
we can still hold them up to our ears
and hear quiet hallelujahs.

the world
is still beautiful.

the new year will gentrify us into better people

the only decision I question from last night
is why I ate so much shrimp and cheese—
and as I smoke this cigarette shirtless
and the air of a brand new year
is gentrifying my chest hair,
all I can say is
I think everything
is gonna be okay.

in fact, this might just be the greatest year
of our lives, because there are cradles
in our hearts and the things inside them
are sniffling and sneezing.
there's a love inside us all
learning how to walk
and maybe, if the chips fall where they should,
that love will walk into our lives
and change us for the better.

you survive until morning by slowly climbing out of the ashtray

after a bad night of drinking
I'm in the backyard acting like a king
holding court with all the discarded cigarette butts
that have suddenly appeared
cause the snow piles are melting
earlier than expected
it's only February but warmer temperatures
have snuck into our shithole
of a snow globe like a terrorist sleeper cell
and the glass is starting to crack all around us
pretty soon we'll be plucking the shards
out of our flesh
losing a little bit of ourselves in the process

oh well, life during wartime
like that Talking Heads song
this ain't no party,
this ain't no disco,
this ain't no fooling around!
but fools are everywhere in this one condom town,
a fool like me
look, I just think it's very important we share
our mistakes with whomever we can
after all self-destructive tendencies
make us beautiful, connecting us in ways
never seen before in human history—
I've always been an optimist, sort of
anyway I try telling the cigarette butts
they have to get their act together

that their chemicals have turned my dad
into a tumor with sad blue collar telepathy
that every night he attaches factory floor bunions
to my brain making my emotions
a little too bony and painful to walk on,
always a rocky ride

I don't know...I try telling the cigarette butts
they're wasting their lives
that apparently 1.7 billion pounds of cigarette butts
litter our oceans and lakes
I saw that on Facebook
but it just makes me think of
mermaid nurses chain smoking
then I imagine there are hospitals hidden
in coral reefs and I think that's beautiful

I'm not getting the message across though;
the butts are lying in the melting snow
not doing anything to make the world a better place
then suddenly in the moonlight
they begin to transform
into everyone I've ever had sex with,
how wasteful it seems
I think it's cause the whole
smoking after having sex thing;
I pride myself on following the rules of intercourse,
being a gentleman about the whole process
that semi-imaginary time we all have in our heads
when chivalry built sprawling skylines
in every american heart
but now that planes fly into buildings,
we're all a little leery of anything that sprawls

I get a text on my phone that says I'm an asshole,
that I got too out of control

look, I've tried my best to be a gentleman,
I drag chivalry like a knight's armor
an emotional rock where everyone
can pull out his or her own personal Excalibur
and know their purpose in life
but every time they pull out the sword
it leaves a wound
and now my insides are looking like vomit
in an ashtray
I like to say this is life in the Rust Belt
but I'm tired of kidding myself

I'll be honest:
I haven't slept in a week,
how am I still functioning?
looking around there seems to be
exploding burlesque dancers everywhere
dangling from tree limbs like pornographic piñatas,

now I know I'm losin' my mind
I just can't get my hormones under control,
flowing through my blood
like Olympic Swimming bedbugs
and the serotonin rashes look like some
unhinged Jackson Pollack painting
and I feel the compulsive need to abort
my body and have my ghost
live out its days in art museums from coast to coast
for patrons to oooh and aaah
at my ectoplasm anomalies

and limbo fault lines,
for them to point and laugh
at my cubist eccentricities,
for young and pretty things with daiquiri brains
to break into tears
and use those tears to fill up water balloons
and throw 'em at me

look, none of us will be able to
Noah's Ark our way out of this flooded mess
this dizzying minstrel show
of living paycheck to paycheck,
parents dying, the system robbing us blind,
earth burning itself out,
too much passion when the girl or boy
in your bed complains of being dead,
when he or she slips into the secondhand sheets
like the world's tiniest violin with unhappy hips
grieving over the guillotine
or that there's no castle being built in the backyard

look, I've tried my best to be a gentleman
but whatever chivalry I can muster
I waste on having to swallow pride
when I pay for coffee with a credit card
or get blowjobs from holes that I dig,
empty burial plots where I spill my seed

look, goodness is a fossil fuel
that burnt out its skeletal wick
thousands of years ago
and on a night like this
when dead cigarettes & climate change
are your only friends

how you survive until morning
is to imagine chivalry tankers leaking in the Atlantic
hit by some iceberg of contempt
and pouring bravery into the blue waters
filling three-eyed fish with purpose
and sharks with a more sacred bloodlust
Great Whites donning business suits
and waiting in line at blood banks in NYC
octopuses declaring love
for all the slit-wristed teenagers
wasting away like starfish
in bedrooms dotting the Rust Belt
or anywhere else in america
how they use their tentacles to suction out stars
from their constellation cubicles
and throw them like Frisbees
through teenage windows
so growing up nowadays
doesn't have to be so damn dark and despairing
you gotta imagine that dolphins
are putting on armor and questing for grails
that whales are cutting open their stomachs
and inviting in all the world's homeless
cause their organs are as good as pillows,
organs as good as bodies of lovers entwined

how you survive until morning
is to foam at the mouth,
to recognize that your heart
is more like the SPCA,
a home for wayward unloved animals,
that sometimes love
lets them roam the streets

biting everyone they see,
recognize you're an animal too

how you survive until morning is opening your eyes
and seeing lonely poltergeists
wearing the tuxes of our forefathers
and strangling club girls with corsages
open your eyes, see all the psychotic paper dolls
uncomfortable in their own skin
hiding out in fitting room bunkers
and waiting for the end of trees

open your eyes,
see gluten free knights jousting
with mirrors in parking lots
hoping to pierce the beating heart
of everything they hate,
too many to list

how you survive until morning is
to convince yourself that the nuclear wasteland
starts on your mattress and spreads
outward like the flu
until the entire world is polluted
by the splitting of your atom,
by the cigarette butts of words left unsaid

how you survive until morning is to dig into yourself
and predict your future
like a whiskey dick Nostradamus,
to free the animals of the zodiac
from the insecure zoo of the mind –

most important though is to see the abyss
for what it is:
it wears a disguise now,
it looks nothing like you'd expect
there's no darkness or emptiness,
it doesn't guzzle down echoes like a porn star
but rather it's fully clothed and has a job,
sneaking into your company
when you least expect
and bringing you down from the inside

how you survive until morning is
having the knowledge that one day
you'll wake up in a cracked snow globe in the middle
of cigarette butts having an orgy
all that waste will be off-putting
not to mention all that coughing flooding your ears
and it'll feel like a train made of swords
is racing up & down your body,
slicing you

but somehow you'll realize
you're wearing a suit of armor,
that none of this matters
that you're strong and unaffectable,
that there's still goodness out there

that you'll find it
even if it kills you

Acknowledgements

Those Who Favor Fire

"These Aren't Mine" and "A Room Full of Mannequins" first appeared in **OCCULUM**

"To Burn a Tree from the Roots Up" and "My Friends" first appeared in **Foundlings Literary Magazine**

"You Become a Flower in the Least Poetic Way" first appeared in **The Magnitizdat Literary**

"Something Wicked This Way Comes" first appeared in **The Buffalo News**

"A Thread" first appeared in the **Karibu News**

"Vaudeville" first appeared in **Ghost City Review**

"To See Them Weightless" first appeared in **My Next Heart: New Buffalo Poetry anthology** (BlazeVOX books, 2017)

"A Bad Taste" and "Pull Your Finger from the Plug" first appeared in **Your One Phone Call**

"7 a.m. in Buffalo" first appeared in **Peach Mag**

Those Who Pray to Fire

"The Last Time I Was Really Happy, Emilio Estevez Was Coaching Peewee Hockey" & "So It Turns out I'm an Asshole Who Has a Cold Sore Fetish" first appeared in **Cease, Cows**

"Cock Cousins Disappearing in the Rust Belt When There's No One Else Left to Fuck" first appeared in **Black Napkin Press**

"Your Melancholy Is Straight out of an Edith Piaf Song," "Gathering Together Dead Body Parts to Assemble the next President of the United States," "We're Living in Closets Full of Snow" & "A Beach Party for Animals That Have Gone Extinct" first appeared in **Zombie Logic Review**

"Picking Fruit off the Sick Future" first appeared in **63 Channels**

"The Green Breast of the New World Is in Allentown" first appeared in **Peach Mag**

"Vomiting into a Toilet Is Democracy in Action" first appeared in **Ghost City Review**

"Self-Destructive People Have a Leg up on Life," "There's No Christmas in the Afterlife," "Elegy for 2016 and Maybe the Death of America" & "The New Year Will Gentrify Us into Better People" first appeared in **Plurality Press**

"The Rise and Fall of the Canalside Christmas Tree" first appeared in **Buffalo Rising**

"Even When We're at Our Worst We're Still Cut from the Same Cloth" & "You Survive Until Morning by Slowly Climbing out of the Ashtray" first appeared in **Foundlings**

About the Authors

Benjamin Brindise strives to be the Swiss Army Knife of poets. Feeling just as at home at a poetry slam in a dive bar in Buffalo, NY as he does as a Teaching Artist as the Just Buffalo Literary Center, or on stage at the National Poetry Slam, Brindise creates work spanning the spectrum from spoken word to the literary page. He encourages his students to be brave in their approach to writing, and tries to do the same himself.
He tweets @benbrindise

Justin Karcher is a poet and playwright born and raised in Buffalo, New York. He is the author of *Tailgating at the Gates of Hell* (**Ghost City Press,** 2015), the chapbook *When Severed Ears Sing You Songs* (**CWP Collective Press,** 2017), and the micro-chapbook *Just Because You've Been Hospitalized for Depression Doesn't Mean You're Kanye West* (**Ghost City Press,** 2017). He is the editor of Ghost City Review. He tweets @Justin_Karcher

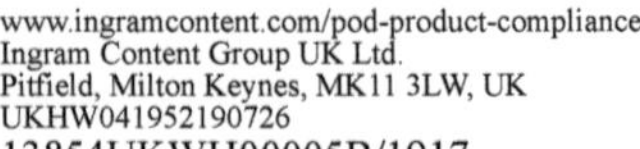

www.ingramcontent.com/pod-product-compliance
Ingram Content Group UK Ltd.
Pitfield, Milton Keynes, MK11 3LW, UK
UKHW041952190726
13854UKWH00005B/1917